D0198378

Ambulance and Air Ambulance Crew

by Nancy Dickmann

raintree

Raintree is an imprint of Capstone Global Library Limited, a company incorporated in England and Wales having its registered office at 264 Banbury Road, Oxford, OX2 7DY – Registered company number 6695582

www.raintree.co.uk
myorders@raintree.co.uk

Produced by Brown Bear Books Ltd:
Text: Nancy Dickmann
Design Manager: Keith Davis
Editorial Director: Lindsey Lowe
Children's Publisher: Anne O'Daly
Picture Manager: Sophie Mortimer
Printed and bound in India

ISBN: 978-1-4747-5547-4 (hardback)
21 20 19 18 17
10 9 8 7 6 5 3 2 1

ISBN: 978-1-4747-5551-1 (paperback)
22 21 20 19 18
10 9 8 7 6 5 3 2 1

British Library Cataloguing in Publication Data
A full catalogue record for this book is available from the British Library.

Acknowledgements
We would like to thank the following for permission to reproduce photographs:
Alamy: Barrie Harwood, 8, Paul Glendell, 19, Peter Manning, 11; Avalon: Photoshot/Cultura 13; courtesy Brackensdale Infant School, Derby, 20; stockphoto: Jeff Fullerton, 5 (top), sturti, cover, 1, 5 (bottom right), 6, 7, 9, 14, 15, 17, 18; courtesy Kingsleigh Primary School, 21; NHS Trust: 16, Yorkshire Ambulance Service , 12; Shutterstock: 1000 words, 4, LandFox, 11

Brown Bear Books has made every attempt to contact copyright holders of material reproduced in this book. Any omissions will be rectified in subsequent printings if notice is given to the publisher. If anyone has any information please contact licensing@brownbearbooks.co.uk

Contents

Some words are shown in bold, **like this**.
You can find out what they mean by looking in
the glossary.

Here comes an ambulance!

An ambulance speeds down the road. Its crew are coming to help people who are ill or injured.

Ambulance and air ambulance crew help people in an **emergency**. They also drive **patients** to **hospital** appointments.

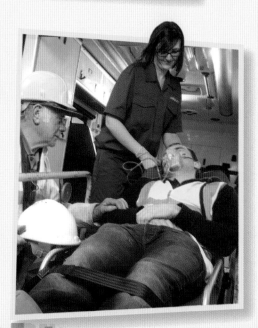

Ambulance crew

For an ambulance crew, every day is different. They never know who will call, or what kind of help will be needed.

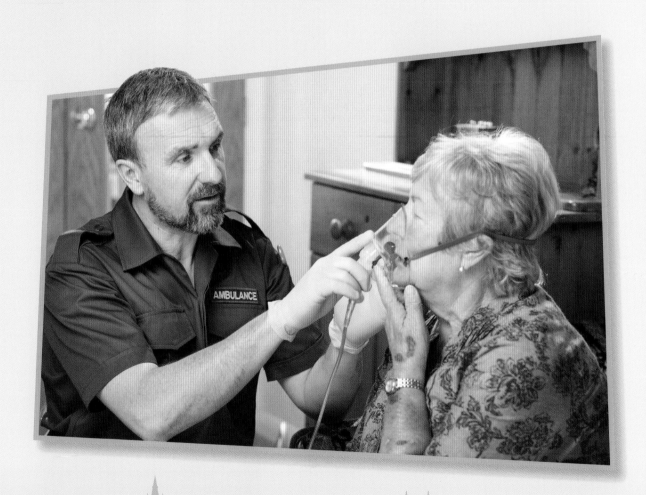

Many ambulance crew members are
paramedics. Paramedics are trained
to give **emergency** care. They may
also drive the ambulance.

On the road

Sometimes a **rapid response vehicle** reaches a **patient** first. A **paramedic** provides care while waiting for the ambulance to arrive.

Rapid response vehicle

Ambulance crew treat patients as soon as they arrive. If patients need more care, the ambulance will take them to **hospital**.

In the air

Some ambulance crew travel by helicopter. They can reach the scene of an accident more quickly. They can reach places where there are no roads.

An air ambulance carries a pilot and
paramedics. They care for people who
are hurt until they can get to **hospital**.

Keeping in touch

In the **control room**, a **dispatcher** answers an **emergency** call. He or she can see which ambulance is closest.

Radio

The dispatcher radios the ambulance.
He or she tells the crew where to go.
The dispatcher will also tell them what
care the **patient** needs.

First aid

Paramedics can help in any situation.
Patients may have been hurt in a fall
or a car accident. They may
be seriously ill.

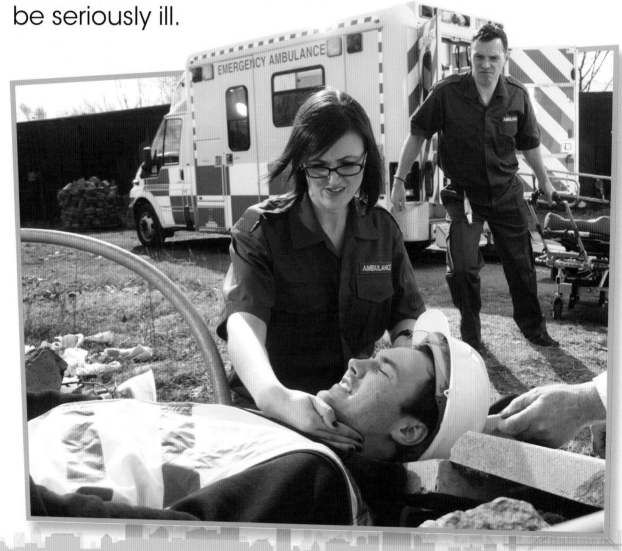

A paramedic stays calm in an **emergency** and provides **first aid**. This includes putting **splints** on broken bones or bandaging wounds. They also give medicines and oxygen.

Inside an ambulance

The driver drives quickly and safely.
Flashing lights and **sirens** warn cars
to get out of the way.

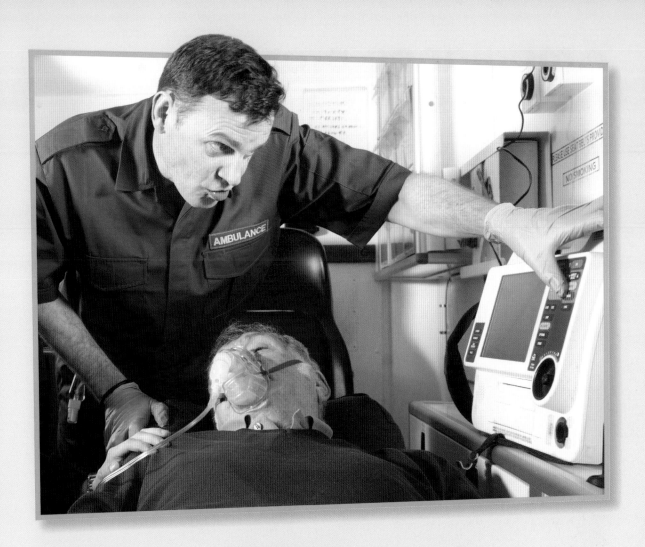

In the back, a **paramedic** stays with the **patient**. The paramedic may radio the **hospital**. He or she tells the doctors what treatment the patient needs.

Ambulance crew uniforms

Most ambulance crew wear a green **uniform**. Sometimes they also wear a **high-vis jacket**.

Most air ambulance crew wear red,
orange or blue. **Paramedics** carry
first-aid equipment in bags. Paramedics
can find what they need quickly.

Visiting schools

Ambulance crew often visit schools.
They talk to children about their job.
They explain how they help **patients**.

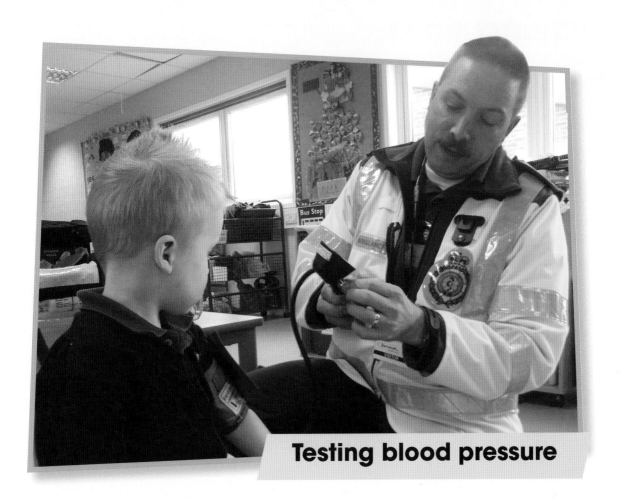

Testing blood pressure

Paramedics talk to children about how to stay safe and healthy. They also teach children who to call in an **emergency**.

Staying safe

Always remember:

⊞ Ambulance crew are there to help.

⊞ You can call 999 in an emergency.

⊞ You will need to tell the dispatcher your address.

⊞ Never call an ambulance unless it is a real emergency.

Glossary

control room where dispatchers answer emergency calls

dispatcher person who answers emergency calls

emergency serious situation that calls for fast action

first aid medical help given while waiting for an ambulance to arrive

high-vis jacket bright jacket that makes a person easy to see

hospital building where doctors care for people

paramedic ambulance crew member who gives first aid until a patient gets to hospital

patient person who needs medical care

rapid response vehicle car or van that is often the first to arrive at an emergency

siren warning device that makes a loud noise

splint device to keep a bone in place while it heals

uniform special type of clothing worn by all members of a group, such as ambulance crew

Find out more

Books

Ambulance Crew (Popcorn: People Who Help Us) Honor Head Wayland, 2013)

Paramedic (Here to Help), Rachel Blount (Franklin Watts, 2016)

Paramedic (People Who Help Us), Rebecca Hunter (Tulip Books, 2014)

Websites

www.bbc.co.uk/news/uk-england-38155471

Watch a video about what's inside an ambulance

www.nwas.nhs.uk/media/1176717/Do-you-know-how-to-call-an-ambulance.pdf

Learn about how and when to call an ambulance

Index